WARNING: **PG 18+**

A STOIC'S GUIDE ON
HOW TO TRAIN YOUR THOTS

H. Azizi

Introduction:

Welcome to a realm where the shadows of humor converge with the jagged edges of reality. This book is not for the faint-hearted, the easily offended, or those who believe in sugar-coating life's brutal truths. **"A Stoic's Guide on How to Train your Thots"** is a satirical exploration that dives headfirst into the depths of masculine stoicism, dark manipulation, biting sarcasm, and relentless wit. It's a collection of jokes and aphorisms that gleefully skewer societal norms, challenge sacred cows, and push the boundaries of what is deemed acceptable.

Dedications:

To all the ladies who have ever struggled with the complexities of modern kitchen appliances:

"They remind us that behind every successful man is a woman who knows her place is near the sink"

~H. Azizi

Summary

Prepare yourself for a no-holds-barred journey through the raw, unfiltered hilarity and brutal honesty of **"A Stoic's Guide on How to Train your Thots"** This is not your average humor book. It's a wild ride, blending masculine stoicism, dark manipulation, biting sarcasm, and relentless wit, all underpinned by timeless Stoic philosophy.

MOTIVATING, FUNNY, AND INSPIRING

Ever wondered what would happen if Marcus Aurelius and George Carlin teamed up for a roast? This book answers that question with a collection of 199 razor-sharp quotes that will have you laughing out loud while contemplating the deeper truths of life. It's like having a Stoic sage and a stand-up comedian in your pocket, ready to dispense wisdom and one-liners at a moment's notice.

From the outrageous to the profound, these quotes are meticulously explained through the lens of Stoic philosophy, proving that even the darkest humor can shine a light on the human condition. Whether it's poking fun at societal norms, dissecting relationships, or just offering a brutally honest look at life, **"A Stoic's Guide on How to Train your Thots"** delivers it all with a punchline.

Why You'll Love This Book

Laugh Out Loud: With a perfect blend of satire, sarcasm, and irony, this book guarantees laughter on every page.

Think Deeply: Each joke is paired with a Stoic insight, making you ponder the bigger picture while you chuckle.

Stay Motivated: The Stoic wisdom sprinkled throughout will keep you grounded and inspired, no matter how chaotic life gets.

Perfect for Fans Of

- Dark humor and witty one-liners.

- Stoic philosophy and timeless wisdom.

- Anyone who enjoys a good laugh while reflecting on life's absurdities.

DISCLAIMER

Table of Contents

THE BATTLE OF THE SEXES

" *F*INISH IN HER", *or whatever Mortal Kombat says:*

Marcus Aurelius might say, "The obstacle becomes the way." A stoic warrior would laugh at the hyperbole and recognize the importance of facing life's trials head-on, with a bit of humor.

"Her: no coochie for you tonight;

Me: no coochie from you tonight":

Epictetus would advise detachment. In relationships, as in all things, the stoic knows that true happiness isn't dependent on external conditions.

"She can unfollow but she can't unswallow":

Seneca might remind us of the permanence of actions and the futility of regret. Once something is done, it cannot be undone – embrace it and move forward.

"Your real ones will have the same frenemies.":

True friendship endures through the same trials and enemies, a concept echoed by Marcus Aurelius.

"Change her mood, not her mind...":

Reflects the idea of controlling what you can. You can't change another's mind, but perhaps you can influence their mood or how you react to it.

"She's not special. You just haven't dated enough women":

Reflects the understanding of impermanence and the importance of experience. Nothing is inherently special, it is our perspective and lack of experience that makes it seem so.

"Don't fix your broken washing machine, file for divorce instead"

Stoicism teaches the importance of endurance and adaptability in the face of life's challenges. Seneca said, "Difficulties strengthen the mind, as labor does the body."

"A man with diabetes is not what she meant when she prayed for a sugar daddy."

This underscores the mismatch between a woman's desire for a wealthy benefactor ("sugar daddy") and the reality she encounters (a man with diabetes). This reflects the Stoic lesson that misaligned or unrealistic desires often result in unmet expectations. Stoicism advises focusing desires on things we can control and finding contentment within those parameters.

WISDOM AND WIT

"Smart people learn from everything and everyone, average people from their experiences, stupid people already have all the answers.":

A quote that echoes Seneca's teaching on humility and constant learning. The wise remain perpetual students.

"Smart people are okay with looking dumb while they figure things out.":

Marcus Aurelius would approve of embracing the process of learning and not fearing the judgment of others.

"Babe you're not an 'empath,' you have PTSD from an unstable household and are sensitive to emotional change as a defense mechanism.":

Wisdom encourages self-awareness and understanding the roots of our behaviors and emotions.

"Hostage or not, sometimes it's nice being held.":

Even in dire circumstances, finding comfort in small things is a way to endure hardship.

"Somewhere between looking out FOR people to looking OUT for people.":

The value & distinction between genuine care and mere appearances, emphasizing the importance of true intentions.

"Before you rush in and save people, make sure you're not interrupting their karma.":

Reflects the belief in the natural order and the importance of letting events unfold as they must.

IRONY AND SARCASM

"*Don't wait for your deathbed to tell people how you feel. Tell them to fuck off now.*":

Epictetus would agree on the importance of living authentically and not postponing what needs to be said.

"*Competition is a low vibe, at the top, we really do be just collaborating.*":

Reflects the ideal of cosmopolitanism – we are all citizens of the world and should work together rather than against each other.

"*The sheep will spend its entire life fearing the wolf, only to be eaten by the shepherd.*":

Marcus Aurelius might point out the futility of misplaced fears and the importance of understanding the true nature of threats.

"If you work from home, you might go multiple days without speaking to another human being, but there are downsides too.":

Highlights the balance one seeks – while solitude is valuable, community and human interaction are also important.

"You're all wrong, the earth isn't round or flat, it's fucked!":

Seneca might see this as a commentary on the state of the world, reminding us to maintain perspective and rationality amidst chaos.

CYNICISM AND STOICISM

"*I can forgive murder but cheating is where I draw the line.*":

This darkly ironic statement might amuse Seneca, emphasizing personal codes of honor and the complexity of human emotions.

"*Does your insurance company know you like being choked while clappin?*":

Reflects the principle of understanding the risks and rewards in life and relationships, with a humorous twist.

"*People muddy shallow water to make it seem deep.*":

A reminder from Marcus Aurelius to see things as they truly are and avoid being deceived by superficial appearances.

"You don't like it when people talk about you, what if they never do?":

Indifference to others' opinions – true peace comes from not needing validation from others.

"I find it amusing that we're all pretending to be normal when we could be insanely interesting instead.":

Encourages embracing individuality and authenticity, key values.

LIFE AND DEATH

"*When the sex is so good you almost go home & tell your wife about it.*":

Highlights the importance of discretion and the value of rational control over impulses. Type Shit

"If you are a rich man who makes money in a dishonorable way, women will forgive this. If you are a poor man who makes little money in an honorable way, women will not forgive this. Women will forgive you for being evil, but not for being powerless.":

Seneca might see this as a commentary on societal values, hypergamy and the illusion of power versus virtue.

"If I die young, I want the boys to post it on their story so girls will slide up out of sympathy and I can be the greatest wingman one last time.":

A darkly humorous take on legacy and reputation, a common concern about how one is remembered.

"It is only when a mosquito lands on your genitals that you realize there is always a way to solve problems without using violence.":

Echoes the principle of finding peaceful and rational solutions to problems.

"If your Tesla gets stolen, it's now an Edison.":

Reflects the idea of impermanence and the fluid nature of ownership and innovation.

SOCIETY AND CULTURE

"Mental health stigma be like: 'it's ok to not be ok' but make sure it's on your time off and it doesn't affect your productivity and you really make up for the inconvenience it created for others and...":

Critique of societal expectations and the call for authenticity and honesty about one's struggles.

"Coincidence is God's way of staying anonymous.":

Reflects the belief in fate and the interconnectedness of all events.

"I think we become whoever would've saved our younger self.":

Emphasizes personal growth and self-improvement, key pursuits.

"Introverts be like 'I know a spot' and then go home.":

A humorous nod to the appreciation for solitude and self-reflection.

"The only difference between a hero & a villain is the villain wants the end to come sooner. Both know it's inevitable.":

Reflects the acceptance of fate and the inevitable end, with differing approaches to life's journey.

ADDITIONAL QUOTATIONS

"*Complacency is Gangster.*":

Stoicism teaches us to avoid complacency and always strive for self-improvement.

"*Evolution formed civilizations, please don't stop.*":

The appreciation for progress and the importance of continuous development.

"*Active voice: I loved your book. Passive voice: Your book was loved. Passive-aggressive voice: I love how you felt the need to write a book.*":

Emphasizes clarity in communication, a virtue.

"Babies kick pregnant women all the time but when nvm.":

Reflects the unpredictability of life and the need to accept it with humor.

"Me in kindergarten after dropping my parents off to work.":

Embracing humor even in life's mundane moments aligns with joy.

"Abusers don't just groom their victims. They also groom their allies to excuse and not question their abusive behavior.":

Understanding the nature of manipulation and maintaining vigilance aligns with teachings.

"The wisest policy of the powerful is to create a kind of pity for themselves as if their responsibilities were a burden and a sacrifice. How can one envy a woman who has taken on a heavy load for the public interest?":

Reflects the idea of masking true intentions and maintaining humility.

"Sad isn't it, how a rich man's joke is always funny, even when it isn't, especially when it isn't.":

Commentary on societal power dynamics and the focus on true value over perceived worth.

"Hear me out, OnlyFans but it's me dressed like your dad and finally telling you I'm proud of you for $7.99/month.":

Highlights the idea of seeking validation from within rather than external sources.

"While you take her on fancy dates trying to impress her, there's a mf out there who lit up one blunt & smashed.":

Reminds us to focus on what truly matters rather than superficial efforts.

"The man who says his girl can't take a joke... she took you bro.":

Emphasizes the importance of humor and resilience in relationships.

"Subtly emphasize how lucky you have been, to make your happiness seem more attainable to other people, and the need for envy less acute. But be careful not to affect a false modesty that people can easily see through. This will only make them more envious & we don't want that now do we?":

Reflects the value of genuine humility and avoiding unnecessary envy.

"The divine plan that the Universe has for you can't be understood by the ego. You can't even comprehend how each and every moment is connected. Everything that you go through is part of a much bigger picture, you gotta tune out of the ego and tune into your higher self to gain clarity. The ego is always confused, it's just trying to survive. It can't go beyond survival, that's what keeps you in fear. Fear clouds your judgment, you mistake redirection for rejection. FOCUS on the bigger picture dammit.":

Encourages detachment from ego and focusing on the broader perspective, a core principle.

"Ignore them so hard they have to run from the police to feel wanted.":

A humorous take on indifference to negative opinions.

"No naked man fears pickpocket.":

Emphasizes the value of simplicity and not being burdened by material possessions.

"If you think only good can come from being insanely skilled at your job then imagine a grief counsellor dies & nobody gives a shit because that's how good he was.":

Reflects the belief in doing one's duty well without seeking recognition.

"I wish guilt triggered before the act.":

A nod to the value of forethought and self-control.

"Saw five people brutally beat up this dude on an electric bike & decided not to help, I think 5 is enough.":

Reminds us to pick our battles wisely and maintain a detached perspective.

"Babe you look the finest in more lighting, angle, distance & long-sightedness.":

Reflects the practice of seeing things as they truly are, beyond superficial appearances.

"My girlfriend just tried to unzip my pants while we were watching a movie... now she's mad at me cuz I said she's gonna miss the movie if she starts doing laundry.":

Highlights the importance of rational priorities and humor in relationships.

"Don't ask them out to dinner, ask them to be your dinner.":

A humorous reminder of the focus on directness and honesty.

"When my girlfriend says, 'Unlock your phone I need to see something.' I just look at her crazy because I don't even let my wife do that.":

Emphasizes the value of trust and boundaries in relationships.

"How many people does it take to screw in a light. Okay but how do you get inside the bulb?":

A playful reminder of curiosity and the importance of asking the right questions.

"She fell in love with a tennis player but love meant nothing to him.":

Reflects the detachment from external validation and the transient nature of emotions.

"Is it just me but when you're in love, day bleeds faster into night, wrong seems right, black looks white, even loose feels tight.":

A humorous take on the understanding of perception and how emotions can alter it.

"Un-Subscribe to their OnlyFans & buy a Gym Membership, you bros worried about the wrong t*tties.":

Encourages focusing on personal improvement and health, aligning with values.

"Al is coming for our jobs' lol I would love to see an Al robot sell adderall to its nephew's friends.":

A humorous reflection on the inevitability of change and the importance of adaptability.

"When your partner tells you they cheated on you, I know there's a temptation to ask 'with who?' Resist it. Instead ask 'with whom?' Speak good English no matter the circumstances.":

Emphasizes the importance of maintaining composure and rationality even in emotional situations.

"Non-existent are the things we have not stubbornly desired yet.":

Reflects the idea that our desires shape our reality.

"Shaking my girlfriend's dad's hand 'Great grip sir I see where she gets it from.'":

A humorous take on the value of respect and acknowledging influences.

"Y'know what's wrong on so many levels? Touching yourself in an elevator.":

A reminder of the importance of self-control and appropriate behavior, key values.

"Life really be having me in the middle of the hood with 100 gang members today and in a boardroom with 10 millionaires tomorrow.":

Reflects the acceptance of life's unpredictability and the ability to adapt to different circumstances.

"Every time you remember... forgive again.":

Emphasizes the practice of forgiveness and letting go of past grievances.

"If there was a line, between right and wrong, I snorted it years ago.":

A humorous take on the exploration of moral ambiguity and personal responsibility.

"A gay dinosaur is called a megasoreass.":

Encourages humor and lightheartedness, even in the face of life's absurdities.

"Therapy is a scam to prescribe you the same drugs with FDA approval.":

A critique on the commercialization of wellness, reminding us to seek true understanding and self-help.

"Always build a new house, if you buy one off the market, make sure the previous owners don't still have the spare keys.":

Reflects the value of prudence and foresight in all endeavors.

"Do not be one of those people who look like paragons of patience but are actually just afraid to bring things to a close: Patience is worthless unless combined with a willingness to fall ruthlessly on your opponent at the right moment.":

Emphasizes the importance of action and decisiveness, key principles.

"You will never understand how sneaky a person is unless you're the side piece, then you prolly know everything.":

A humorous reminder of the importance of awareness and understanding human nature.

"Bros, be sure to find women who will appreciate your work, make you laugh, trust you & spoil you, just make sure they never meet each other.":

Reflects the value of balance and managing relationships wisely.

"Instead of regretting that you can't wake up age 18 again, pretend to yourself that you're 90 and you've woken up age 37 again, and that you get to magically, wonderfully have the next 50 years.... again.":

Encourages living in the present and appreciating the gift of life, a core belief.

"The deadline, then, is a powerful tool. Close off the vistas of indecision and force people to make up their damn minds or get to the point, never let them make you play on their excruciating terms. Never give them time.":

Reflects the value of decisiveness and the importance of setting boundaries.

"Bros, if she says she can change you, hold her close, look deep in her eyes & shit your pants.":

A humorous take on the value of authenticity and resisting unnecessary change.

"Turned my Happy meal upside down cuz it really be a Sad meal at this age.":

Embraces the acceptance of life's phases and finding humor in aging.

"Who wudda thought 5 years ago that 8 hours of sleep now would be the greatest achievement.":

Highlights the importance of appreciating simple pleasures and self-care, aligning with values.

"You remind me of my lil toe cuz I wanna hit you on every table I see.":

A playful reflection on irritation and maintaining humor in relationships.

"The worst part about kissing a perfect 10 is how cold the mirror feels on my lips.":

Encourages self-love and humor about narcissism.

"Bros, if he can't fight, she's single.":

Reflects the value of strength and readiness to protect what matters.

"Women deserve equal rights... & Lefts.":

A controversial statement highlighting the value of equality and the importance of respectful discourse.

"If you are not fed love with a silver spoon, you will learn to lick it from knives.":

Reflects the idea that hardship can teach resilience and resourcefulness.

"I took an elective called 'Stress', foolishly thinking I was going to learn about meditation and yoga. Instead the professor spent 6 weeks proving that being poor or a minority literally destroys your health on a molecular level, and I think about that every day.":

Highlights the importance of understanding the impact of societal issues on personal well-being.

"All navy men were once semen.":

A playful reminder of the humble beginnings and evolution, reflecting the value of growth.

"Smoking Kills? If you want their sales to plummet, stop encouraging people.":

Encourages rational decision-making and understanding the consequences of actions.

"Apparently these days when you donate, it's gotta be your blood.":

A humorous critique on societal expectations and the value of true generosity.

"Alpha males', I hear that in the context of software, where alpha versions are unstable, missing important features, filled with flaws, and not fit for the public.":

Encourages humility and the importance of continuous improvement.

"Fear you'll need all that you can get.":

Reflects the value of preparedness and facing challenges head-on.

"Blocked her with the same thumb I had in her.":

Emphasizes the importance of boundaries and detachment in relationships.

"Girls want a strong brother. Sons want a strong father. Women want a strong husband; But your side fade's gotta be on point for all that rizz you throw for validation.":

Reflects the value of strength and the importance of maintaining appearances.

"I just accidentally, prematurely sent a work email to a supplier. It was supposed to say 'I am afraid that we will have to reschedule our meeting.' I hit send when all it said was: 'Hi Dave, I am afraid.'":

Encourages acceptance of mistakes and maintaining composure in all situations.

"Bros, even if she has a boyfriend or a husband, if another man's value is high enough, she will consider him. Understand Hypergamy, you're welcome.":

Reflects the understanding of human nature and the importance of self-awareness.

"Women like men with money. Men like women with an hourglass figure. She's not a 'gold digger', and you're not a 'pig'. Stop trying to fight human nature.":

Emphasizes the value of acceptance and understanding human desires.

"If it weren't for physics and law enforcement, I'd be UNSTOPPABLE.":

Highlights the importance of respecting laws and the limitations of human capabilities.

*"The past is returning to see if you grew up or not...
Don't fold.":*

Reflects the value of learning from past experiences and not repeating mistakes.

"Can't gaslight me. I'ma just agree with you. you think I'm crazy? tbh same.":

Emphasizes the importance of maintaining composure and rationality in the face of manipulation.

"When setting out on a journey, do not seek advice from those who have never left home.":

Encourages seeking wisdom from those with experience, a key principle.

"Dwayne Johnson can become a lesbian because rock always beats scissors.":

A humorous take on the value of strength and resilience.

"Corruption is sometimes sentenced in life but always punished in the life after, you can finesse law just not divinity.":

Reflects the belief in natural justice and the importance of integrity.

"I went to a feminist rally & came back with my shirt ironed holding a sandwich.":

A humorous critique on societal expectations and the value of individualism.

"Her new man wasn't new man you just never knew man.":

Reflects the value of clarity and understanding in relationships.

"Because you achieve your accomplishments with grace and ease, people believe that you could always do more if you tried harder. This elicits not only admiration but a touch of fear. Your powers are untapped - no one can fathom their limits.":

Encourages humility and the importance of continuous self-improvement.

"Treating all women equally is a disrespect to high quality women.":

Highlights the value of discernment and respect.

"Prepare and prevent so you don't have to repair or repent.":

Reflects the value of foresight and preparation.

"Just realised all men are feminists, apparently you gotta tap into your masculine energy to become one.":

Encourages balance between masculine and feminine energies, aligning with values.

"Men have the biggest & strongest egos, which they are entitled to wear/pull off if they have the work ethic & vision to back it up.":

Emphasizes the importance of backing up confidence with hard work and vision.

"You think men abuse substances every now and then to look tough & shit? I've seen a bunch of grown-ass men regroup like minions to 'discuss the situation' when the plug introduced new prices.":

Highlights the importance of rational discussion and adaptability in challenging situations.

"A man's family is a reflection of him. Impressive man = impressive family. Unimpressive man = unimpressive family. If you want to know who you are, look at the people around you to see your reflection.":

Reflects the value of self-awareness and the importance of one's influence on their surroundings.

"We tend to want the world to know what we have done, we want our vanity gratified by having our hard work and cleverness applauded, and we may even want sympathy for the hours it has taken to reach our point of artistry. Learn to control this propensity to blab.":

Encourages humility and the importance of inner satisfaction over external validation.

"Email me for free consultation on how to cure your PMS for 9 months.":

A humorous take on the value of offering help and understanding.

"Never date a woman who disrespects your wife.":

Reflects the Stoic value of respect and loyalty in relationships.

"Step dads are the type of men women would never date if they didn't have children.":

Emphasizes the importance of recognizing the roles and contributions of individuals in different contexts.

"Never expose the sweat and labor behind your poise. Some think such exposure will demonstrate their diligence and honesty, but it actually just makes them look weaker, as if anyone who practiced and worked at it could do what they had done.":

Reflects the value of maintaining composure and not seeking unnecessary validation.

"Omw home today, witnessed a black cat cross my path and then get run over by a truck right after.":

Highlights the acceptance of fate and the unpredictability of life.

"If you think you read more than me just know I used to make my librarians blush.":

Encourages the pursuit of knowledge and the importance of intellectual humility.

"The fate of those who do not make others dependent: Sooner or later someone comes along who can do the job as well as they can, someone younger, fresher, less expensive, less threatening & better.":

Reflects the value of maintaining relevance and not relying on others' dependence.

"And that's the problem with people who mean everything they say, they think everyone else does too.":

Encourages discernment and understanding that not everyone operates with the same level of sincerity.

"I opened my mouth, almost said something. Almost. The rest of my life might have fumed out differently if I had. But I didn't.":

Highlights the value of thoughtful speech and the power of restraint.

"Everyone talks about how social media is bad for your mental health but what about Excel?":

A humorous critique on modern stressors and the importance of balancing work and well-being.

"You've heard of fomo now get ready for fobi (fear of being included).":

Reflects the value of independence and not being swayed by societal pressures.

"If your friend Jack was stuck on a tree would you help your friend Jack Off?":

A playful reminder of the importance of helping others while maintaining a sense of humor.

"Plug: I'm at the park in a red hat next to the kids play area. Me: Okay, look left that's me coming down the slide.":

Emphasizes the value of maintaining playfulness and joy in everyday interactions.

"Me: What do you want? Wife: A divorce.

Me:

Wife:

Me: into drive thru speaker 2 Happy Meals Plz...":

Highlights the importance of humor and resilience in the face of personal challenges.

"Yes, English can be weird. It can be understood through tough thorough thought, though.":

Encourages the appreciation of language and the importance of clear communication.

"Trauma can freeze a part of you at the age it happened. That means that a part of you might still be frozen at that age and feel as if that trauma is still happening now. It's possible to be an adult with a much younger part of you running your life, business or relationship.":

Emphasizes the importance of self-awareness and healing past traumas.

"All women have pussies bro, don't give her another one to deal with.":

Reflects the value of respect and understanding the importance of supporting others rather than adding to their burdens.

"[Conceal intentions with false sincerity) Espouse a belief in honesty and forthrightness as important social values. Do this as publicly as possible. Emphasize your position by occasionally divulging some heartfelt thought, though only one that is meaningless or irrelevant.":

Encourages genuine sincerity and the importance of integrity.

"Truth is men can fake a relationship for a climax & women can fake a climax for a relationship.":

Reflects the value of authenticity and the importance of genuine connections.

"My secret joy is seeing people graduate from art school and enrolling in coding bootcamps 2 years later.":

Highlights the importance of adaptability and the pursuit of practical skills.

"The most powerless thing a person can do is let an inconsistent partner know they will stay, waiting for them to reach the potential they do not have.":

Emphasizes the value of self-respect and the importance of not settling for less than one deserves.

"I know my exes see me and be like, 'I hate that sexy mf'.":

Encourages self-confidence and the importance of moving forward from past relationships.

"These bros be lying to women about inches & then complaining why they're so bad at parking.":

Highlights the importance of honesty and self-awareness in relationships.

"Distance yourself only to find out I'ma better shot at distant objects.":

Reflects the value of perspective and the importance of taking a step back to gain clarity.

"The most intriguing individuals embody paradoxes: scholars with strength, affluent in simplicity, and warriors of the spirit.":

Encourages the cultivation of diverse qualities and the importance of balance in personal development.

"Work like a slave till you own one.":

Reflects the value of hard work and perseverance in achieving one's goals.

"Finally killed my ego, now I'm better than everyone who hasn't yet.":

A humorous take on the practice of humility and the importance of overcoming ego.

"Do you guys see somebody spell a word wrong & look down at the keyboard to see how close the letter is to the letter that's supposed to be there, to see if it's socially acceptable to misspell said word, or are you normal?":

Encourages attention to detail and the importance of clear communication.

"It can take years to tame a wild beast, but it takes only seconds to become one.":

Reflects the value of self-control and the importance of vigilance.

"Weak fathers give rise to misguided children, misguided children become horrible parents, horrible parents raise a broken generation. Strong fathers are the only cure for society.":

Emphasizes the importance of strong leadership and positive influence in families and society.

"Trust me, the reward ain't shit without the struggle.":

Highlights the value of perseverance and the importance of embracing challenges.

"The best part about duct tape is that it turns a 'Nooo!' in to a 'MmMMM!'.":

A humorous reminder of the value of resourcefulness and finding solutions.

"Children, you're here because your dad's not queer. Happy Father's Day.":

Encourages the appreciation of family and the importance of honoring one's parents.

"Most of the time, when people make mistakes, they genuinely intended to do something good. Focus on that intention and try to understand the motivation behind it. Once you can empathize with their motivations, you'll find it easier to forgive them & yourself.":

Reflects the practice of empathy and the importance of understanding and forgiveness.

"Police: When did you realize your wife was dead? Me: wiping tears the lovemaking was same but then the dishes started to pile up.":

Highlights the importance of humor and resilience in the face of personal challenges.

"The first name on your driver's license & the last name on your birth certificate is your gay name.":

A playful reflection on identity and the importance of self-acceptance.

"Don't objectify women, tell her she belongs to you.":

Encourages respect and the importance of genuine connections in relationships.

"Me: I'm so excited for this date. I've been saving all week. Her: I really don't mind splitting the bill. Me: The bill?":

Reflects the value of generosity and the importance of mutual respect in relationships.

"Women sleep with who they want. Men sleep with who they can. Men marry who they want. Women marry who they can.":

Emphasizes the understanding of human nature and the importance of self-awareness.

"Doc: How's your headache?

Me: She's alright.":

Highlights the importance of humor and resilience in personal challenges.

"Me changing my voice every time the pretty blind girl rejects me."

Encourages adaptability and the importance of maintaining a sense of humor in relationships.

"Despite being the reason, I'll still hold your hand if you can't walk properly the next day.":

Reflects the value of loyalty and the importance of supporting loved ones.

"It might pass like a kidney stone, but this too shall pass.":

Emphasizes the acceptance of temporary pain and the importance of endurance.

"Plastic flowers don't grow when you water them.":

Highlights the importance of focusing on what is real and genuine, a key value.

"Bros, they age like milk, you age like wine, you're the prize, not them.":

Reflects the value of self-respect and the importance of recognizing one's worth.

*"Listen, you're a ghost driving a meat-coated skeleton made from stardust & clay, walking a rock, hurtling through space & time continuum, fear no man, trust no b*tch.":*

Encourages a cosmic perspective and the importance of fearlessness, a core principle.

"Indians suck at football because every time they get in a corner they open a store.":

A humorous critique on stereotypes and the importance of recognizing cultural differences.

"No one drives a stolen car gently, they will hit the acceleration at max, be rough with it on the road, countless rounds with it, only abandon it when the gas tank is empty.":

Reflects the value of responsibility and the importance of treating possessions with care.

"It's in your best interest to allow the significance of her character to reveal itself.":

Encourages patience and the importance of truly understanding others.

"Disney doesn't have the balls to put a black man on screen acting like a monkey, that's why Tarzan will always be white.":

Highlights the importance of recognizing and challenging racial stereotypes.

"The razor blade is sharp but can't cut a tree; the axe is strong but can't cut hair, never look down on anyone unless you're admiring their penis.":

Encourages humility and the importance of recognizing everyone's unique strengths.

"If I've offended you with my posts, I apologize... I didn't know you could read.":

A humorous reflection on the importance of not taking offense easily.

"Microplastics found in male genitalia for the first time, researchers raising concerns over choking hazards for your mom.":

Highlights the importance of environmental awareness and the consequences of pollution.

"If a woman asks if you 'notice anything new' tell her 'I do, your beauty surprises me every day.' Then continue thinking about velociraptors.":

Encourages the value of maintaining focus and finding humor in everyday interactions.

"Before the invention of the crowbar, crows drank at home.":

A playful reminder of the importance of innovation and the value of simplicity.

"Treating kids decently doesn't mean identically, there are no bad kids just bad parents.":

Reflects the value of fairness and the importance of nurturing positive development.

"You can't scare me, I used to hold the fleshlight for my dad.":

Emphasizes the value of resilience and the importance of overcoming challenges.

"I bought my daughter a handbag from Iraq. She said thanks for the Baghdad.":

A humorous take on the importance of gratitude and cultural awareness.

"Some guy once woke up and said let me pull some cow titties... imagine how many things he sucked until he found cow milk.":

Reflects the value of perseverance and the importance of discovery.

"She will malfunction if you keep mixing the colors & the whites.":

Highlights the importance of understanding and respecting individual differences.

"If a lot of women touch your glass of water, you can clean it and drink from it, but if a lot of men dip their fingers in it, it'll be too nasty to drink.":

Reflects the value of cleanliness and the importance of maintaining standards.

"Judge a book by its cover ~ graphic designer.":

Encourages the importance of first impressions while also understanding deeper value.

"If humans can't see air, can fish see water? But since humans can see water, can fish see air?":

Reflects the value of curiosity and the importance of understanding different perspectives.

"Every store is a museum if you are poor enough, every museum is a store if you are rich enough.":

Reflects the understanding of perspective and the value of appreciating what you have.

"Nut together n call it an ourgasm type shit.":

A playful reminder of the value of unity and shared experiences.

"Don't knock on a deaf man's door forever.":

Emphasizes the importance of recognizing when to move on, a key principle.

"People can't eat opinions, that's why they call them assholes.":

Reflects the value of practicality and the importance of focusing on what truly matters.

"Like Hellen Keller at an orgy, you dunno who you're fuckin' with.":

A humorous reminder of the importance of awareness and understanding one's situation.

"I know your parents think I am a bad influence, please be obedient & collect your allowance."

This quote humorously captures the essence of influence and perception, key areas explored in Stoic philosophy. Here's how we can relate it:

"Say No to Sleep, Wait Instead."

Epictetus emphasized the importance of self-discipline and control over one's desires and impulses. He said, "No man is free who is not master of himself."

"I once punched so fast, it broke the speed of light."

The exaggerated claim of breaking the speed of light by punching humorously highlights human tendencies to boast and inflate our achievements. A Stoic would encourage recognizing our true capabilities without resorting to hyperbole, promoting a balanced and humble self-view.

"Impregnate the system."

Marcus Aurelius, emphasized the importance of taking meaningful actions within the framework of the world we inhabit. Marcus Aurelius wrote, "Waste no more time arguing about what a good man should be. Be one."

"The umbrella becomes a burden to carry when rain stops."

This teaches us to avoid unnecessary attachments and to let go of things that no longer serve a purpose in our lives. Epictetus advised, "Don't cling to things that are not truly your own. They are given to you for the time being, not forever."

"You look like you gamble on farts & lose."

This shows the importance of exercising good judgment and avoiding unnecessary risks. Seneca advised, "We should be wary of unwise actions that, if they go wrong, can result in shame or harm."

"Call them your world, then talk about your ambition for world domination."

This advises us to value our relationships and to treat others with respect and care. Marcus Aurelius wrote, "Love the people with whom fate brings you together, but do so with all your heart."

"Changing the word 'bitch' to 'fridge,' cuz some of y'all be takin' too much meat."

This emphasizes the importance of moderation and self-control in all aspects of life. Epictetus taught, "Freedom is not procured by a full enjoyment of what is desired, but by controlling the desire."

"Been witnessing people losing their minds over things they didn't bring to the world with them."

This quote resonates strongly with Stoic principles about attachment, the impermanence of external things, and the importance of focusing on what is truly within our control. True peace comes from within and that external possessions and circumstances should not dictate our inner state. Epictetus famously said, "Wealth consists not in having great possessions, but in having few wants."

The quote highlights the irrationality of becoming overly attached to material possessions or external circumstances things we didn't have when we were born and won't take with us when we die. Stoicism advises cultivating an attitude of detachment towards these things, recognizing that they are transient and ultimately outside our control.

"Girls can talk boys out of ambition."

Suggests that external influences, such as relationships or others' opinions, can sometimes lead us away from our ambitions. A Stoic would argue that while relationships are important, one should not let external influences distract from one's path to virtue and self-improvement. The Stoic approach would be to recognize these potential distractions and maintain focus on what truly matters: one's own actions, goals, and character.

"If I were in your shoes, I'd take them off 'cause life's a beach."

A laid-back approach to life, akin to enjoying the moment and not being overly burdened by unnecessary concerns ("take them off 'cause life's a beach"). Stoics advocate for appreciating the present moment and not being overly worried about what lies beyond our control. Just as one would relax at the beach, Stoicism encourages a mindset where we can find calm and contentment no matter the circumstances.

"I have a wet dream that maybe one day we will all take a shower."

The dream of everyone "taking a shower" conveys the idea of a shared, collective goal. In Stoic philosophy, the betterment of the individual contributes to the betterment of society as a whole. The quote, in a tongue-in-cheek way, suggests that if everyone focuses on their own "cleanliness" (or virtue), the whole community benefits.

"Pullout game better than King Arthur."

The "pullout game" is for precise timing and quick decision-making. In Stoicism, acting with precision and timing is a virtue; making decisions at the right moment is essential for a virtuous life. Just like King Arthur pulling the sword at the right time, this modern metaphor suggests the importance of acting with deliberate intent.

"My teachers raise their hands to speak to me."

The reversal of roles in the quote suggests that traditional hierarchies do not necessarily determine who has the true authority. In Stoic philosophy, the wise person understands that real authority comes from virtue and knowledge, not just from titles or positions. The quote serves as a reminder to respect wisdom wherever it is found, not just from those in traditional positions of power.

"You will never see things you're not looking for."

This implies that if you're not actively looking for something, you'll never notice it. This aligns with the Stoic principle that we must consciously direct our attention to what truly matters. Our thoughts and perceptions shape our experience of reality, so being intentional about what we choose to focus on is key.

"Been witnessing people losing their minds over things they didn't bring to the world with them."

The irrational behavior of becoming overly distressed about things that were never truly ours to begin with—"things they didn't bring to the world with them." In Stoic philosophy, this behavior is seen as a failure to understand the nature of ownership and control. We come into the world with nothing, and we leave with nothing, so fretting over temporary, external things is contrary to Stoic wisdom.

CONCLUSION

"A Stoic's Guide on How to Train your Thots" is a wild ride through the labyrinth of human nature, where every turn reveals a new facet of our collective psyche. It's a book that doesn't just laugh at the absurdities of life but embraces them with a knowing grin. Enjoy the journey, and remember, sometimes the darkest places are where the brightest insights can be found.

YOU'RE WELCOME
Follow the Author for more updates!

@AZIZISOFTWAREGUY

www.ingramcontent.com/pod-product-compliance
Lightning Source LLC
Chambersburg PA
CBHW051551120626
46551CB00013B/1468